# How To ~~Pass~~ BLIT
# ABRSM Theory
## Grade 5

## by Samantha Coates

**Chester Music**
part of The Music Sales Group
London / New York / Paris / Sydney / Copenhagen /
Berlin / Madrid / Hong Kong / Tokyo

Published by
Chester Music,
part of The Music Sales Group,
14-15 Berners Street,
London W1T 3LJ, UK.

Exclusive Distributors:
Music Sales Limited
Distribution Centre, Newmarket Road,
Bury St Edmunds, Suffolk IP33 3YB, UK.

Music Sales Pty Limited
4th floor, Lisgar House,
30-32 Carrington Street,
Sydney, NSW 2000, Australia.

Order No. CH85668
ISBN 978-1-78558-491-6

Printed in the EU.

Your Guarantee of Quality:

As publishers, we strive to produce every book
to the highest commercial standards.

Particular care has been given to specifying acid-free, neutral-sized
paper made from pulps which have not been elemental chlorine bleached.

This pulp is from farmed sustainable forests and was
produced with special regard for the environment.

Throughout, the printing and binding have been planned to ensure
a sturdy, attractive publication which should give years of enjoyment.

If your copy fails to meet our high standards,
please inform us and we will gladly replace it.

www.musicsales.com

# A Note From the Author

Dear theory student,

Congratulations! You have just done the very best thing for your theory education — you've bought this book.

There are quite a lot of new things to learn in Grade 5, but what you really need to know is that this book builds on the knowledge you gained in Grades 1-4. If you are 'jumping in' at Grade 5 level because you have a practical exam coming up, there will be many things you need to brush up on. All of this is outlined on page 5, but the best strategy is to work through the workbooks from previous grades before you start this book. Discuss this more with your teacher, of course.

Every time you see this icon:  it means there are extra resources available on the website.

Go to www.blitzbooks.com to download free worksheets, flashcards, manuscript and more!

Happy theory-ing,

Samantha

It takes more than an author and a publisher to produce a book — it takes enormous support from friends and family. Thank you to everyone who has helped me on the BlitzBooks journey, but most of all to Andrew, Thomas and Courtney... without you three, there would simply be no books.

# Contents

# Things You Should Know From Grades 1-4

←———————————————————————————————————————→

You'll need to do a crash course on this stuff with your teacher if you are jumping in at Grade 5 level! (The best way to do this, of course, is to work through How to Blitz! ABRSM Theory Grades 1-4)

**KEY SIGNATURES:** Major and minor keys with up to five sharps or flats, and the major and minor scales of these keys, as well as chromatic scales starting on any note.

**TIME SIGNATURES:** All simple and compound time signatures.

**NOTE VALUES:** All note and rest values from breve down to demisemiquaver, double-dotted notes, duplets, and the correct groupings of notes and rests within time signatures.

**TERMINOLOGY:** Names of ornaments, technical scale degree names, e.g. supertonic.

**CLEFS:** Recognising notes in the ALTO clef (in addition to treble and bass).

**OTHER STUFF:** You'll also need to know how to go about any of the following tasks, because these could easily crop up in your Grade 5 exam!

★ Write major, minor (both forms) or chromatic scales in any of the set keys/clefs

★ Rewrite melodies in any of the set clefs either at the same pitch or up/down an octave, sometimes converting from accidentals to key signature and vice versa

★ Fix beaming and grouping in rhythmic exercises containing errors

★ Compose a four-bar rhythm

★ Compose a rhythm to suit the words of a poem

★ Rewrite melodies with notes of half or twice the value

★ Convert rhythms from simple to compound and vice versa

★ Write and recognise chords I, IV and V in root position in any of the set keys/clefs

★ Name any interval by number and type, including diminished and augmented intervals

★ Answer general questions about standard orchestral instruments

★ Recognise ornaments and signs, and translate all the Italian (and French) terms you learned in Grades 1-4! (These can be downloaded from **www.blitzbooks.com**)

Got all that? Woo hoo you're ready to tackle Grade 5! Turn the page!

# New Sharp Keys

Our new sharp keys for Grade 5 are F♯ major and its relative D♯ minor. These keys have SIX sharps! Here is the key signature in the treble clef. Rewrite it in bass and alto clefs:

 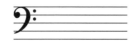 

You'll remember from Grade 4 that G♯ minor needed a **double sharp** ( 𝄪 ) to raise the leading note. Well, D♯ minor is the same:

Look! The 7th note is already a C sharp! Add a double sharp here

Write a D♯ melodic minor scale below, using semibreves. Write the key signature, and write one octave ascending and descending. (You'll need to use a single sharp to cancel the double sharp on the way down.)

Now write an F♯ major scale, one octave descending, using accidentals instead of a key signature (also in semibreves). Check the clef!

Write these key signatures and scale degrees (again, in semibreves). Watch out for clef changes!

| B major | A major | C♯ minor | D♯ minor |
|---------|---------|----------|----------|
| supertonic | submediant | subdominant | leading note |

Write the tonic (I), subdominant (IV) and dominant (V) triads in root position in our two new keys with six sharps in the key signature. Check the clefs, and don't forget to raise the leading note in chord V of D♯ minor!

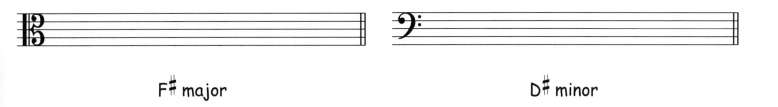

F♯ major                                             D♯ minor

Here is a melody with lots of sharps.

Beethoven

What key is it in? (Hint: bar 1 centres around the tonic, and the melody contains E sharps.) _____

Rewrite the melody here, using a key signature instead of accidentals:

Name this scale:

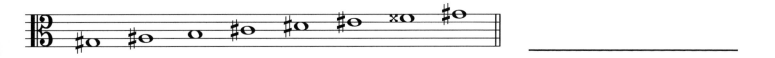

_____

For your final trick using sharps, write a one-octave ascending **chromatic** scale beginning on F♯. Use semibreves, and write the scale in any clef you like!

# New Flat Keys

Our new flat keys for Grade 5 are G♭ major and E♭ minor. These keys have SIX flats! Here is the key signature in the bass clef. Rewrite it in alto and treble clefs:

   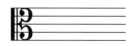   

Write an E♭ melodic minor scale here, using semibreves. Write the key signature, and write one octave ascending and descending. Check the clef!

Now write a G♭ major scale, one octave descending using accidentals (also in semibreves). Check the clef!

Name these key signatures. The note in each bar is the **mediant** of that key.

_____   _____   _____   _____   _____

Write these key signatures and scale degrees. Watch out for clef changes!

| B♭ major | E♭ minor | B♭ minor | C minor |
|----------|----------|----------|---------|
| supertonic | leading note | dominant | leading note |

Write the tonic (I), subdominant (IV) and dominant (V) triads in root position in our two new keys with six flats in the key signature. Once again, check the clef and be careful with the leading note!

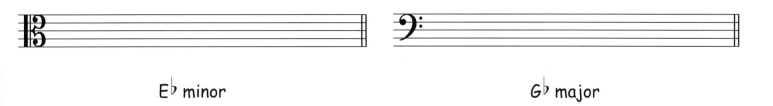

Eᵇ minor                                             Gᵇ major

Here is a melody which features a bunch of flats:

Chopin

What key is it in? (Hint: make a list of all the flats, in key signature order. It's a minor key.) _____

Rewrite the melody here, with a key signature instead of accidentals (don't forget, you may need to include accidentals for a raised 7th degree):

Now write it AGAIN, in the alto clef (with the key signature), sounding one octave lower.

DID YOU KNOW... our new keys with six sharps/flats are **enharmonic equivalents** of each other. Go and play all the scales you wrote on page 8 followed by the scales you wrote on page 6. They sound exactly the same!

# Tenor Clef

In Grade 4, you learned about the alto clef, which looks like this: 𝄡. It is also known as a **C clef**, because it indicates where middle C lies in the stave.

In alto clef, middle C is on the third line: 𝄡 𝅝

Now we're going to learn about another C clef! It is called a **tenor clef**. It looks just like an alto clef, but it is raised up by one line. It's kind of like an alto clef filled with helium!

The tenor clef shows middle C on the fourth line: 𝄡 𝅝    Wow! This is MIDDLE C! And yes, tenor clef is supposed to stick up above the stave a bit

So 𝄡 𝅝 sounds exactly the same as this 𝄞 𝅝 and this 𝄢 𝅝 !

Draw a whole load of tenor clefs here. Make sure they're all centred on the fourth line:

The tenor clef is mostly used by cello, bassoon, and tenor trombone (more about these instruments on pages 63–67) because of the range they often play in. Here is 'Twinkle, Twinkle, Little Star' written in A major, at the same pitch in four different clefs. (Check out the look of the key signatures!) You can see that alto and tenor clefs are easier to read because there are no leger lines. Can you finish off the tune in the other three clefs?

Key signatures look rather different in tenor clef, especially sharp keys:

Check this out! The sharps go in the opposite zig zag dirrection!

Write these key signatures in tenor clef:

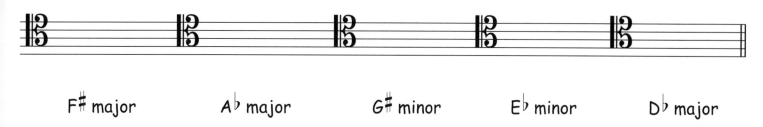

F♯ major        A♭ major        G♯ minor        E♭ minor        D♭ major

Rewrite the following notes in tenor clef, keeping the pitch the same. All you need to do is keep the position of middle C (shown in grey) in your head at all times.

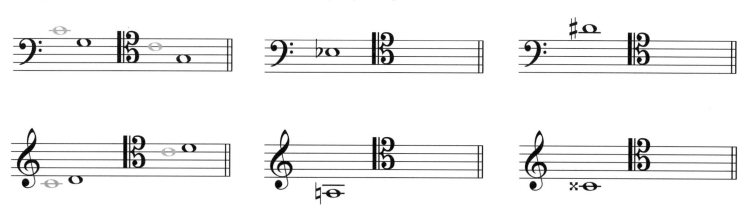

Rewrite these short Mozart melodies:

1. In tenor clef, keeping the pitch the same. Remember to write the key signature.

2. In treble clef, sounding one octave **higher**. First, work out the starting note at the same pitch, then put it up an octave!

11

# Irregular Time Signatures

In Grade 5 we study four irregular time signatures: $\frac{5}{4}$, $\frac{5}{8}$, $\frac{7}{4}$ and $\frac{7}{8}$. They are irregular because the top number cannot be divided evenly by two or three. This means you'll see a mixture of groups of twos and threes in the same bar!

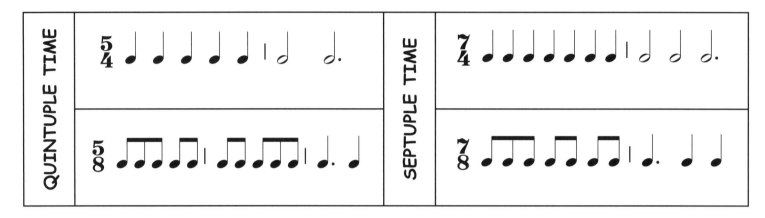

(The table above shows just a few of the many possible combinations in these time signatures!)

Write the correct time signatures for these one-bar rhythms (and yes, they're all irregular):

Insert the correct time signature AND the missing rests at the places marked *:

Bennett

REMEMBER: these new time signatures are in addition to all the time signatures you learned in Grades 1–4!

12

The following extracts change time signatures at each place marked with an asterisk.
Insert the correct time signature, choosing from the list below:

$$\frac{7}{4} \qquad \frac{7}{8} \qquad \frac{5}{8} \qquad \frac{5}{4} \qquad \frac{3}{8} \qquad \frac{2}{4} \qquad \frac{7}{64} \qquad \frac{3}{2} \qquad \frac{4}{4}$$

Bartók

Bartók

Mussorgsky

Bartók

DID YOU KNOW... time signatures with a 5 on top are called 'quintuple' time, and time signatures with a 7 on top are called 'septuple' time! Cool, huh?

13

# More Irregular Things

In Grades 3 and 4 you learned about triplets (three notes played in the time of two) and duplets (two notes played in the time of three). Well, there are even more unusual ways to group notes within a beat!

A group of five, six or seven notes, with that number written across the beam, is equal to FOUR notes of that value. Check these out:

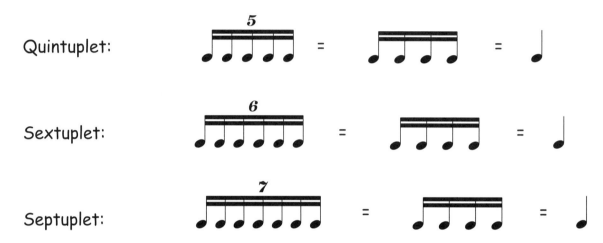

Quintuplet:

Sextuplet:

Septuplet:

A run of nine notes is equal to EIGHT of the same value. So:

**HERE'S A THOUGHT:** The quintuplets, sextuplets and septuplets above are written as semiquavers, and are equal to one crotchet beat. But if they were grouped with one beam only, i.e. as quavers, each group would be equal to four quavers... which is a minim beat!

Insert the correct time signature for these one-bar rhythms:

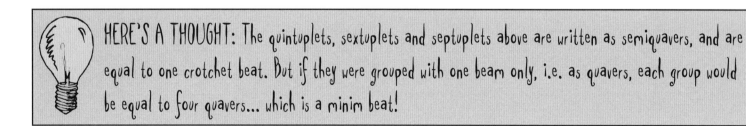

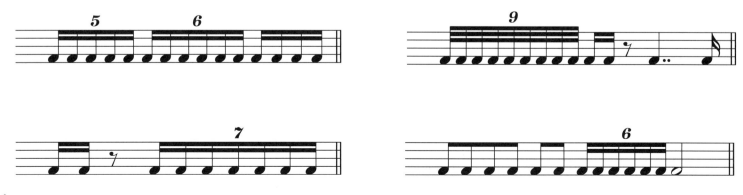

# Not Your Regular Quiz (get it?)

1. Check out this piece by Chopin and answer the questions below.

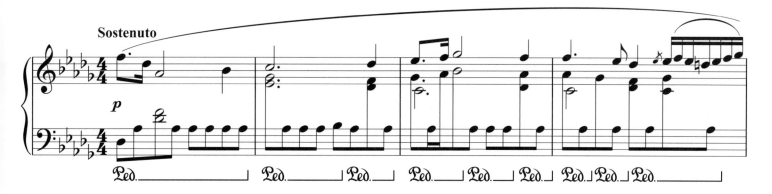

a) Write the correct number above the irregular group of semiquavers.

b) How many quaver beats would that group be worth? _____

c) What is the key of the piece? _____ (Hint: the right-hand part begins on the mediant)

d) What does 'sostenuto' mean? _____

2. a) Insert the correct time signature for this extract by Bartók:

   b) Name the accents: _____

3. Add the time signature for this piece, also by Bartók (who was clearly very fond of irregular things):

4. How many minims is [9-note group] worth? _____ (Hint: the answer is a fraction)

# Compound Intervals

IMPORTANT: Before you go on, make sure you have revised all your Grade 4 interval skills!

Any interval that spans more than one octave is called a **compound** interval. It has the same number and type as if it were one octave smaller, so:

If [score] is a major 2nd, then [score] is simply a **compound** major 2nd!

To name any compound interval, simply move the top note down an octave or the bottom note up an octave, then work out the number and type.

Name these intervals, remembering to put the word 'compound' before each:

_____  _____  _____  _____

The other way to name an interval spanning more than an octave is to keep counting the distance between the notes, i.e. instead of 'compound major 2nd' you'd get 'major 9th'. This can really start to add up though, like in this Beethoven melody:

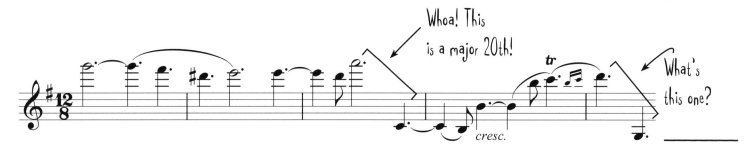

Whoa! This is a major 20th!

What's this one?

HOT TIP: No matter which naming system you choose, it's ALWAYS easiest to first rewrite the interval so that both notes are within an octave, before you try to figure out the number and type.

Complete the table on the next page (which uses a technique we learned in Grade 4) for great practice in naming compound intervals!

16

| 'Dressed' compound interval | Draw it within an octave and without accidentals ('undress' it) | Name the 'naked' interval | Describe how the accidentals affect the interval | Now name the original interval! |
|---|---|---|---|---|
| *(bass clef notation)* | *(bass clef notation)* | minor 2nd | top note is one semitone higher, bottom note is one semitone lower, therefore the interval is two semitones larger | compound augmented 2nd |
| *(treble clef notation)* | *(treble clef notation)* | | | |
| *(bass clef notation)* | | | | |
| *(treble clef notation)* | | | | |
| *(bass clef notation)* | | | | |

Don't forget: if you need to identify intervals from a piece with a key signature, you'll need to rewrite the interval with accidentals first. For example, simply convert *(notation)* into *(notation)*, then work out the name of the interval using the process above!

Describe fully the intervals (by number and type) marked with brackets in this melody:

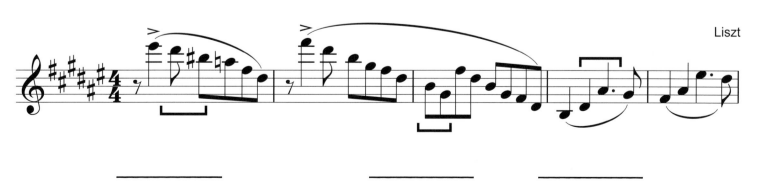

Liszt

_____        _____        _____

# Intervals and Things

Name the intervals marked A, B and C with brackets. Remember, it's easiest to rewrite compound intervals within an octave, and with accidentals instead of a key signature, to work out the number and type. If you need spare manuscript go to **www.blitzbooks.com**.

Interval A _____          Interval B _____          Interval C _____

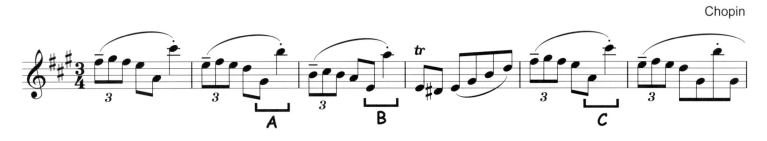

Interval A _____          Interval B _____          Interval C _____

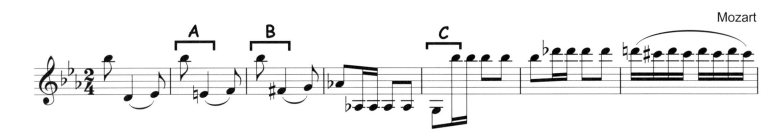

Interval A _____          Interval B _____          Interval C _____

Interval A _____          Interval B _____          Interval C _____

On this page you have to name the intervals AND insert the missing time signature for each example! There are also some Bonus Things To Do (after all, this isn't called Intervals and Things for nothing).

Saint-Saëns

Interval A _____     Interval B _____     Interval C _____

Bonus Thing To Do: Add the missing triplet signs in bar 2.

Rimsky-Korsakov

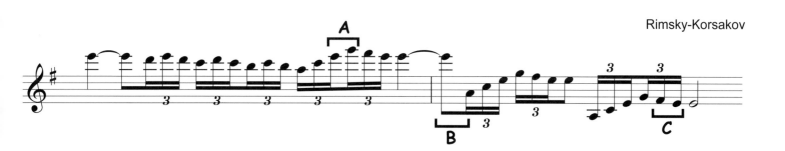

Interval A _____     Interval B _____     Interval C _____

Bonus Thing To Do: True or False: The first tied note is equal to a dotted crotchet. _____

Fauré

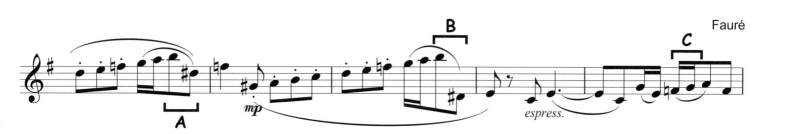

Interval A _____     Interval B _____     Interval C _____

Bonus Things To Do:     Is the time signature simple or compound? _____

Is it duple, triple or quadruple? _____

What does 'espress.' mean? _____

19

# Let's Test Your Skills So Far

Here are two pieces of music and a whole load of questions to answer on each. You'll need to use all of the skills you've learned so far in this book (plus ALL the skills you learned in Grades 1-4, of course!).

Mussorgsky

★ Name the two possible keys of the extract above: _____ and _____

★ Insert time signatures at the places marked *

★ Rewrite the first two bars an octave lower, using the tenor clef. Remember to include the key signature.

★ Write as a breve the enharmonic equivalent of the third note in bar 1.

★ True or false: the left-hand part consists entirely of octaves. _____

★ Name and explain the signs on the notes in bars 1 and 2: _____

★ Who wrote this music? _____ (not difficult, if you're observant)

★ Fully describe the interval marked with the letter Y in bar 4: _____

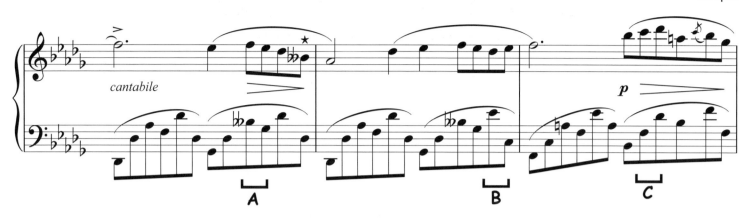

★ The key of this piece is ___ minor. Write one octave ascending of that scale here, using semibreves. Use accidentals instead of a key signature.

★ What is the relative major key of the scale you just wrote? _____

★ Write as a breve the enharmonic equivalent of the note marked *.

Watch out! Key signature here!

★ Insert the correct time signature (hint: it's compound time)

★ Name the ornament in bar 3: _____

★ Ignoring that ornament, rewrite bars 2 and 3 of the treble melody, using notes of HALF the value. Write the key signature, the new time signature, and make sure you group the notes correctly.

★ What does 'cantabile' mean? _____

★ Fully describe the intervals marked with brackets under the bass stave. (Be careful! They are VERY tricky, because of the key signature! You may want to rewrite them with accidentals, on spare manscript.)

Interval A _____        Interval B _____        Interval C _____

# Transposing Instruments

Most instruments of the orchestra are non-transposing, which means they sound at **concert pitch**. For example, when flutes play a C, it actually comes out sounding like a C. This means:

Flute music that looks like this  sounds like this

You may be thinking, 'that's SO obvious, why are we even discussing this?'! Well, it's because not all instruments behave like that! Some instruments are **transposing instruments**.

## INSTRUMENTS IN B FLAT (e.g. clarinet in B flat, trumpet)

When these guys play a C, they get the sound of... B flat! This is why they are called 'instruments in B flat' (and it's due to the convoluted evolution of these instruments, which we won't go into right now). So:

Trumpet music that looks like this  sounds like this

★   Instruments in B flat sound a major 2nd ( __ semitones) lower than written.   ★

## INSTRUMENTS IN A (e.g. clarinet in A, cornet in A)

When these guys play a C, the get the sound of... A! So, for instruments in A:

Music that looks like this  sounds like this

★   Instruments in A sound a minor 3rd ( __ semitones) lower than written.   ★

And finally...

## INSTRUMENTS IN F (e.g. horn, cor anglais)

When these guys play a C, they get the sound of... you guessed it... an F! So:

Horn music that looks like this  sounds like this

★   Instruments in F sound a perfect 5th ( __ semitones) lower than written.   ★

The way music is written for transposing instruments is called **written pitch**. The way it sounds is called **concert pitch**. Can you fill in the rest of the concert pitch notes?

| | Written pitch (i.e. what they play) | Will actually sound | Concert pitch (i.e. what we hear) |
|---|---|---|---|
| Instruments in B flat | *(music notation)* | Down a major 2nd | *(music notation)* |
| Instruments in A | *(music notation)* | Down a minor 3rd | *(music notation)* |
| Instruments in F | *(music notation)* | Down a perfect 5th | *(music notation)* |

**HOT TIP:** When transposing from concert pitch to written pitch, all the notes will go UP a major 2nd / minor 3rd / perfect 5th!

Some instruments are called transposing instruments but do not actually change key. They simply sound an octave higher/lower than written. For example:

**Piccolos** sound an octave **higher** than written. (Can you fill in the sounding pitch?)

Their music looks like  but sounds like

*some serious leger lines needed here*

**Double basses** sound an octave **lower** than written.

Their music looks like  but sounds like

Did you know, there are quite a few more transposing instruments than are listed here? Can you research and list three? _____, _____ and _____.

# More about Transposing

When transposing from written pitch to concert pitch and vice versa, the rhythm and shape of the transposed melody must be the same as the original. However, lots of the time the accidentals will CHANGE! (Veeeery tricky)

For example, here is a melody in C major. In bar 2, you'll see it has a sharp which is straight away cancelled by a natural:

If we wanted a clarinet in B flat to make the sound of the melody above, we have to transpose it **up a major 2nd**, to D major. You'll notice that the accidentals remain the same (fill in the missing notes, which should all be two semitones higher than the original):

But what if the C major melody WAS the written pitch? To get concert pitch, we would have to transpose it **down a tone**, to B flat major (fill in the missing notes, all a tone lower). As you can see, in this version the accidentals CHANGE:

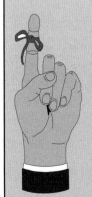

The most important thing to remember is that accidentals do a job:

A sharp sign (♯) always **raises** a note by one semitone

A flat sign (♭) always **lowers** a note by one semitone

A natural sign (♮) could be raising **or** lowering a note – it depends on the key signature – or it could be cancelling out a sharp or a flat!

# Adjusting Accidentals

Each of the following melodies has been transposed for you (hooray!) except for the accidentals (boo). Work out what 'job' each accidental is doing: write 'R' for raised and 'L' for lowered on each one. Then add the correct accidentals to the transposed melodies!

HOT TIP: when transposing a perfect 5th up or down, remember that B to F is not a perfect 5th! B up a perfect 5th is F♯, and F down a perfect 5th is B♭.

Transpose these yourself! First, label the accidentals, then write the new notes, then adjust the accidentals where necessary.

25

# Transposing Tricks

Here is a cool trick to help you find the new notes in your transposed melody. You can write a table that shows you how each note changes. For example, if your original melody has two sharps in the key signature, write the letter names of the MAJOR scale with two sharps:

| Original key: **D major** | D | E | F♯ | G | A | B | C♯ | D |
|---|---|---|---|---|---|---|---|---|

Let's say you have to transpose it up a minor 3rd. Find the MAJOR scale of the note a minor 3rd (three semitones) higher: F major! Write these letter names directly below the D major letter names.

| Original key: **D major** | D | E | F♯ | G | A | B | C♯ | D |
|---|---|---|---|---|---|---|---|---|
| Up minor 3rd: **F major** | F | G | A | B♭ | C | D | E | F |

Now you can see that D will become F; E will become G; F♯ will become A (not A♯!), etc.

Let's test this out with a melody in D major, so that we can use the table above. First, label all the accidentals with 'R' or 'L', just like we did on the previous page:

Now transpose the melody up a minor 3rd (to be written for, say, cornet in A). Write the new key signature, and move all the notes. Remember to use the table above to help! (Remember that you won't actually need to write a flat sign next to the Bs in your transposed melody, because you'll have a key signature.)

Now copy 'R' and 'L' in all the same spots, and adjust all the accidentals according to those labels. (Be careful when raising the Bs – you'll need a natural!) Yay, your melody is transposed!

> HOT TIP: If you're transposing using key signatures, you can actually write your transposing table without any sharps/flats against the letter names. You'll still need to label and adjust all the accidentals!

You can use transposing tables in any situation. If the given melody has no key signature, simply assume it's C major! Let's try it with this melody by Brahms. Transpose it up a perfect 5th, as it would be written for horn. (But first, label the accidentals, of course!)

| Original key: **C major** | C | D | E | F | G | A | B | C |
|---|---|---|---|---|---|---|---|---|
| Up perfect 5th: **G major** | G | | | | | | | |

Now write the new key signature and transpose the melody. (And, of course, remember to add the 'R' and 'L' labels and adjust the accidentals.)

Occasionally the exam question can be a bit tricky. You're given a melody with a key signature, and asked to transpose it WITHOUT using a key signature! Just write your table very carefully, including all sharps/flats in the new scale, and follow it to the letter (ha ha).

This is the cor anglais part from music by Bizet. Write it as it would sound at concert pitch.

Assume the key is major

| Original key: _____ | |
|---|---|
| Down perfect 5th: _____ | |

Include all the accidentals shown in the table, THEN make the adjustments.

That's it! You're now a transposition expert!

# Let's Transpose

1. These are the actual sounds made by a horn in F. Transpose this to its written pitch, i.e. up a perfect 5th. Write the new key signature.

Chopin

2. This melody is in written for clarinet in A. Write the melody in concert pitch, i.e. down a minor 3rd, without a key signature.

Tchaikovsky

3. Here is another melody by Tchaikovsky, written at concert pitch. Rewrite it for clarinet in B flat, i.e. up a major 2nd. Write the new key signature.

# A Bit of Revision

1. Write the scale of D♯ melodic minor:

   ★ use a key signature

   ★ use crotchets

   ★ write one octave ascending and then descending

2. Transpose this melody so that it is at written pitch for cornet in A (so, up a minor 3rd).

3. Write the following key signatures and the named scale degree for each.

| F♯ major | A minor | D♭ major | C♯ minor | E♭ minor |
|---|---|---|---|---|
| submediant | leading note | subdominant | dominant | leading note |

4. Fill each of these bars with **one sound**. (Hint: you may need to use tied notes in some of them!)

# Chord II

In Grade 4 we studied the three primary triads: chords I, IV and V. Now we're going to add chord II! It's the SUPERTONIC chord, which of course is built on scale degree no. 2.

N.B. We always use Roman numerals when referring to chord numbers. For now, the numerals are always upper case. In higher grades, you'll learn about lower-case numerals.

Each of these chords is the supertonic triad of its key. Name each key.

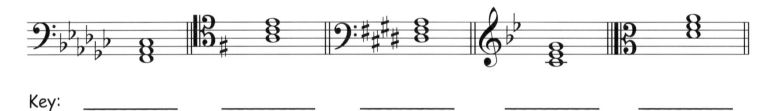

Key: _____    _____    _____    _____    _____

Label each chord marked with an asterisk below as I, II, IV or V. They are all in root position, so you really only need to look at the bottom note of each chord!

Your hint for identifying the key: the piece ends on the tonic chord.

Welsh ballad tune

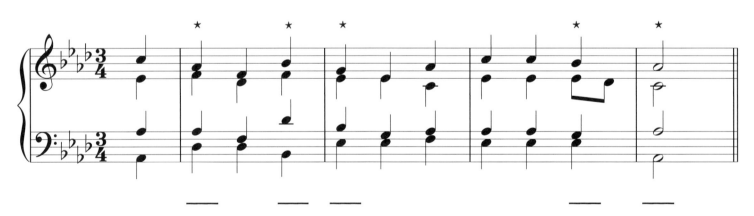

Write chord II in root position in the named keys. Use accidentals. Watch out for clef changes!

C minor          A major          G major          F minor          F# minor

# First and Second Inversion

Up until now we've only dealt with triads in root position, i.e. the root of the chord is the bottom note, and the 3rd and 5th of the chord sit above it.

C major triad, root position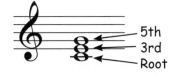

Here's the thing – if we change the order of the notes, we get two different **inversions**:

C major triad, first inversion

**First inversion** means that the **3rd** of the chord is the bottom note

C major triad, second inversion

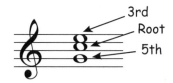

**Second inversion** means that the **5th** of the chord is the bottom note

There are two shortcuts for naming the position of any chord. The first is to use the letters a (root position), b (first inversion) and c (second inversion) after the Roman numeral. So, if you are referring to chord IV in second inversion, you can just call it IVc!

The other shortcut is to use **figures**. Root position is called $\frac{5}{3}$, first inversion is called $\frac{6}{3}$ and second inversion is called $\frac{6}{4}$. These figures refer to the intervals above the bass note:

Root position ( $\frac{5}{3}$ )     First inversion ( $\frac{6}{3}$ )   Second inversion ( $\frac{6}{4}$ )

| 3 ways to name chords! | Words | Letters | Figures |
|---|---|---|---|
| (staff, Root) | Root position | a (e.g. Ia) | $\frac{5}{3}$ (e.g. I$\frac{5}{3}$) |
| (staff, 3rd) | _____ inversion | b (e.g. Ib) | $\frac{6}{3}$ (e.g. I$\frac{6}{3}$) |
| (staff, 5th) | _____ inversion | c (e.g. Ic) | $\frac{6}{4}$ (e.g. I$\frac{6}{4}$) |

# More on Chord Positions

The bottom note of ANY chord tells you its position, no matter what order the other notes are in! Here is the tonic chord of G major, in various positions. Write the letters a, b or c next to each Roman numeral to show the position. (The first one is done for you, yay)

Chord I of G major consists of the notes G, B and D in any order.

B is the bottom note here, which means this chord is in first inversion!

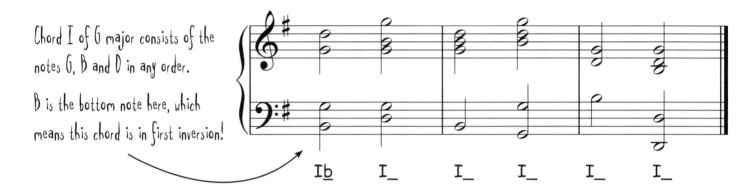

Ib    I_    I_    I_    I_    I_

Let's do that again, this time using figures! These chords are all chord IV of A major.

Chord IV of A major contains D, F and A (and sometimes the A might be missing).

The bottom note is the one that tells you the position of the chord.

$IV^5_3$    IV☐    IV☐    IV☐    IV☐    IV☐

Here is a chord progression in B♭ major, with chord numbers underneath (and the notes of that chord written above, just to help out a bit). Can you label the position of each chord? You can use letters OR figures – choose a method and stick to it!

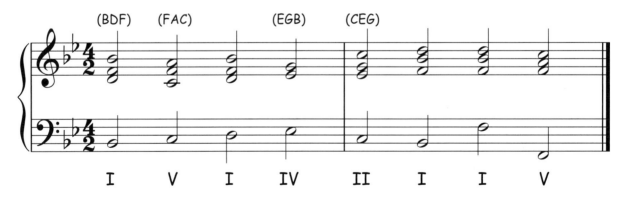

(BDF)    (FAC)    (EGB)    (CEG)

I    V    I    IV    II    I    I    V

The positions of the last two chords in the example above form a really important chord progression in music. Chord I in second inversion followed by chord V in root position is often referred to without Roman numerals and is known as the $^6_4$ $^5_3$ progression. It always occurs on the dominant note of the key. More about this later!

# Identifying Chords

There is a super easy way to identify any chord and its position. All you need to do is draw a little grid containing the letter names of chords I, II, IV and V (in root position order) in any particular key. For example, complete this C major grid:

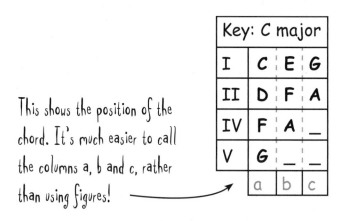

This shows the position of the chord. It's much easier to call the columns a, b and c, rather than using figures!

## Things to Notice

★ There are three columns of letter names

★ Column a shows the **root** of each chord.

★ Column b shows the **3rd** of each chord.

★ Column c shows the **5th** of each chord.

So, this grid is going to help us identify the chord **number** by matching up the letter names, and the chord **position** by checking whether the bass note comes from column a, b or c!

Let's identify this chord. The key is D minor, so first we have to write a D minor grid!

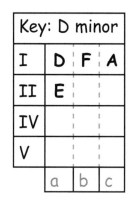

1.  List the notes you see in the chord. Ignore repeated notes. _____

2.  Which chord number in the grid contains those notes? _____

3.  Does the **bottom note** of the chord come from column a, b, or c? _____ That means this chord is in root position / first inversion / second inversion (circle correct answer)

4.  So the final answer is: _____. Easy! (IIb? Or not IIb? That IS the question. Ha. Ha ha. Ha ha ha ha.)

HOT TIP: You'll get used to reading your grids quickly the more you practise. The rows tell you the chords and the columns tell you the positions! Write out grids in lots of different keys.

# Let's I.D. Chords

In case it's not completely obvious from the title of this page, identify each chord marked with an asterisk, naming the chord number and its position. You can choose to use letters or figures to name the position (hooray).

To make it easy, complete a chord grid in the key of each new extract below (they are all major keys, hooray again).

All of the extracts contain the $\frac{6}{4}$ $\frac{5}{3}$ (Ic – Va) progression we talked about earlier. Put a circle around these two chords when you find them!

| Key: | | | |
|------|---|---|---|
| I | | | |
| II | | | |
| IV | | | |
| V | | | |
| | a | b | c |

Traditional

Traditional

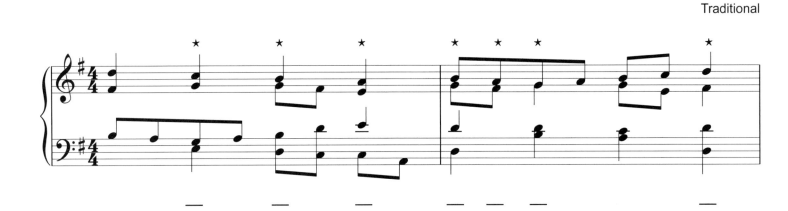

Rowlands

# SATB: Choir Music

The letters SATB stand for the four voices in a choir – soprano, alto, tenor and bass.

The highest voice is called SOPRANO
The second-highest voice is called ALTO
} ← *These are usually female voices*

The second-lowest voice is called TENOR
The lowest voice is called BASS
} ← *These are usually male voices*

Soon you'll be writing melodies for voice, so it's important to know the typical ranges used in vocal music:

In real life many singers can reach notes well outside these ranges! However, you can be sure that if you stick to these ranges when writing for voice you won't put anyone outside their comfort zone.

Sing some songs with your teacher. Which vocal range is best for you? _____

 DID YOU KNOW... Female voices with a range in between soprano and alto are called 'mezzo-soprano'. Male voices with a range in between tenor and bass are called 'baritone'. Interesting, huh?

Name the type of voice that best suits these melodies, given the range of notes:

Saint-Saëns

Voice: _____

Puccini

Voice: _____

# Short Score vs Open Score

SATB music can be written two different ways: **short score** and **open score**.

**Short Score** is written on two staves bracketed together. The two higher voices are written on the treble stave and the lower voices on the bass stave. There are special rules in short-score writing:

S.
A.

Soprano and alto voices are always written in the treble clef. The soprano stems go UP, and the alto stems go DOWN.

T.
B.

Tenor and bass voices are always written in the bass clef. The tenor stems go UP, and the bass stems go DOWN.

Did you read that stuff about stems carefully? Stems follow special rules in short score so that it's easy to follow each part, and so that the stems don't crash into each other! Most of the time the stems are going in the wrong direction according to the normal rules.

Add stems to the four parts in these chords. (Remember, going from top to bottom it's up—down—up—down)

In short score, if two voices sing the same note, it has to be made obvious that there

are two parts. You'll either see two stems on one note, like this:  , or two notes

written side by side, like this ⬚ if they have different rhythmic values, or this

⬚ if both parts sing notes that have no stems!

**Open score** is written on FOUR staves bracketed together. Each voice gets its own line!

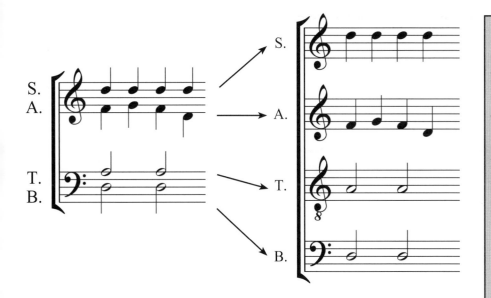

**OPEN SCORE RULES**

★ each voice gets its own stave

★ stems revert to normal (phew!)

★ the tenor part is written **an octave higher**, in the treble clef! (See the little 8 hanging off? This clef is called 'octave treble clef'. Notes in this clef sound an octave lower.)

Here is a passage by Purcell that shows four vocal parts (open score) and a piano part at the bottom that is actually the same notes written in short score. Fill in the missing bars, converting the parts from short to open score and vice versa! Remember, you will have to:

★ (short score to open score) write the tenor part **up an octave**, in the octave treble clef

★ (open score to short score) write the tenor part **down an octave**, in the bass clef

★ make sure the stems are following the rules for short/open score!

# Let's Score

In your exam you'll have to convert short score to open score and vice versa. Let's practise!

Watch out for the unison parts in this first extract, adapted from Attwood.

Schumann

Have you checked and double-checked all your stems???

Oh, sorry, but there's still more on this page. At least you'll be an expert by the end!!!

40

# Short Score and More

1. This music adapted from Schubert is in the key of ___ major. Label the chords marked with an asterisk.

2. Now rewrite the soprano part up a minor 3rd.

3. What is the name for the vocal range between soprano and alto? _____

4. What is the name for the vocal range between tenor and bass? _____

5. Study this excerpt by Dvořák and answer the questions below.

a) What does lento mean? _____ What does ♪ = 112 refer to? _____

b) There is an irregular time division in this melody. Find it and write the correct number underneath.

c) Name two ornaments in this extract. _____

d) Look ahead to the instrument ranges on pages 63-67. Name three instruments that could play this piece: _____

Awesome work!

# Another Short Test

As usual, answer questions about this music.

Monti

1. Which two instruments is this music mostly likely written for? _____ and piano.

2. Ignoring the ornaments, rewrite the solo part from the beginning until the end of bar 2 in the **treble** clef, sounding one octave higher. Write the key signature.

3. They key is G minor. Bar 1 of the piano part consists of chord I. Which inversion is played in the right hand? _____

4. Working from your answer to question 2 above, transpose it down a major 2nd, as it would sound if played by a clarinet in B flat. Write the new key signature.

5. Find and circle the $^{6\ 5}_{4\ 3}$ (Ic - Va) chord progression in this traditional music:

**RESULT: BLITZED IT / PASSED / TRY AGAIN** (circle correct answer)

42

# Cadences

A cadence consists of two chords that finish off a musical phrase. On the next page we'll be talking about cadences in melodies. In Grade 5 we study three types of cadence. Here's an example of each, in C major:

**PERFECT CADENCE**

The **perfect cadence** consists of chords **V – I**. It is like a musical full stop. A LOT of pieces end with a perfect cadence!

**IMPERFECT CADENCE**

The **imperfect cadence** consists of **any chord leading to chord V**. Since chord V sounds very unfinished, the imperfect cadence is like a question mark in music. (II–V shown here, but I–V and IV–V are also imperfect cadences!)

**PLAGAL CADENCE**

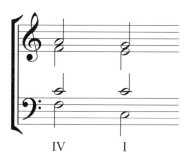

The **plagal cadence** consists of chords **IV - I**. It is very common to hear this at the end of a hymn (the 'amen' bit), after the perfect cadence. Think of a plagal cadence as a few words in brackets after you've made your final point.

Complete this table:

| NAME OF CADENCE | CHORDS USED | DESCRIBE IN PUNCTUATION TERMS |
|---|---|---|
| | V – I | |
| Imperfect | | |
| | | An extra comment after final point |

DID YOU KNOW... There is a fourth type of cadence, called an 'interrupted cadence'. It consists of chords V–VI. This cadence is like a musical semicolon! You'll be learning more about this cadence in higher grades.

# Melody Writing

In your exam you will have to write a melody. This is a new and exciting skill! Even if you've never composed a melody before, you can make it sound good by following a few guidelines. Let's start by studying this melody in C major. Play it, or ask someone to play it for you:

## Things to Notice

★ The melody is based on chords – one chord per bar.

★ There are two phrases: the first phrase ends on chord V (forming an _____ cadence), and the second phrase ends on chord I (forming a _____ cadence).

★ The chord I bars mostly contain the notes C, E and G.

★ The chord V bars mostly contain the notes G, B and D.

Put a circle around C, E and G in the chord I bars, and circle G, B, and D in the chord V bars. We'll call these circled notes 'chord notes'. (We'll call two consecutive chord notes a 'chord jump'.)

## Passing Notes

As you can see, there are some notes in each bar (the notes without a circle!) that do not belong to the chord. These are called 'passing notes'. Passing notes give the melody interest and variety. Here are two important rules for passing notes:

1. Don't leap to or from passing notes. They must be sandwiched between chord notes.

2. They sound best on weak beats, letting the chord notes fall on the strong beats.

Here is a melody with only chord notes. Play or sing it through – you'll find it's a bit boring! Make it more exciting by adding a few passing notes. You'll need to turn some of the crotchets into quavers to do this! (And remember, you may not leap to or from a passing note!)

Here's a rhythm for you to write your own melody in G major. Clap through the rhythm and decide on the phrasing. Mark two phrases with slurs.

Now write a melody below, following these steps:

1. Use one chord per bar. The easiest chord sequence for now is I – V – V – I.

2. Work out which notes are in chords I and V in G major. Write these note names above the bars so that you know which notes you'll be using the most.

3. Compose your melody using a mixture of chord notes and passing notes. **Use chord notes on the strong beats of the bar.** It's also a good idea to use chord notes for longer note values. Make sure passing notes only occur on weak beats.

4. Whenever you use the leading note, it MUST go up to the tonic, unless it is part of a downward scale passage.

5. Make sure your melody ends on the tonic, and mark the phrasing.

Sometimes your melody will have an anacrusis. The best note to use for this is the dominant (scale degree no. 5). Try a melody in F major to this rhythm (follow the steps above):

Circle the chord notes in your melodies. **They should all occur on the beat.** The uncircled notes are passing notes; make sure you haven't jumped to or from a passing note!

 Go to www.blitzbooks.com for more worksheets on melody writing!

# More on Melody Writing

In Grade 5 you have to set words to music, and your melody may end up being four or eight bars long. Composing a melody for someone to sing is more involved than just choosing notes. We're going to look at two eight-bar settings of this couplet:

> Hummingbirds flutter with grace round the field
> The place so serene with such beauty to yield

## Setting 1

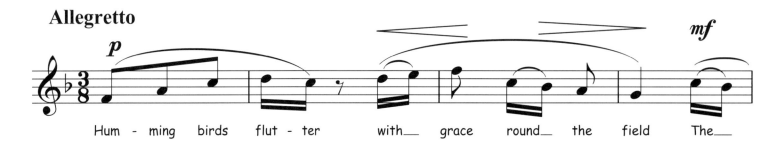

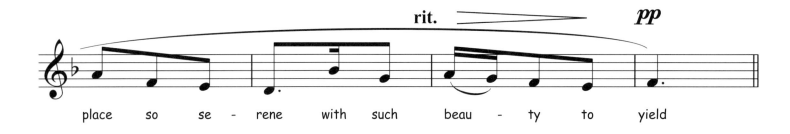

## Good Things to Notice about Setting 1

★ The melodic range suits a soprano voice very well.

★ The melody reaches chord V at the halfway point.

★ The treatment of the word 'flutter' is a great example of word painting, i.e. the faster note values suit the words.

★ The melody has a smooth shape. The leap of a 6th in bar 6 is resolved inwards.

★ It has a good mixture of chordal movement and passing notes.

★ Sensitive phrasing, tempo and expression markings have been added.

# Setting 2

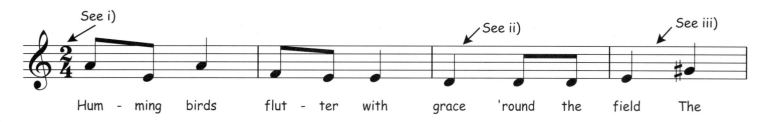

Hum - ming birds flut - ter with grace 'round the field The

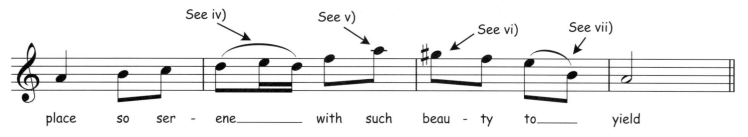

place so ser - ene\_\_\_\_ with such beau - ty to\_\_\_\_ yield

# Not-So-Good Things to Notice about Setting 2

i)   A march-like time signature of $\frac{2}{4}$ does not suit these words

ii)  Repeated notes hold up the flow of the melody.

iii) The rhythm here, and in fact throughout all of bars 1-4, is very boring.

iv)  On a word like 'serene', it's not a good word painting to suddenly have semiquavers.

v)   The range of the melody extends too high for a standard soprano vocal range.

vi)  The awkward interval of an augmented 2nd is difficult to sing. The melodic form of the minor scale should have been used here.

vii) The rhythm of the text is awkward here, e.g.

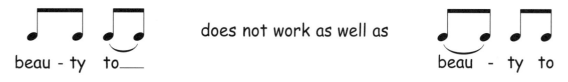

beau - ty to\_\_\_     does not work as well as     beau - ty to

(Try to give small words like 'to', 'a' and 'the' smaller note values)

viii) And... there is no phrasing, dynamics or any other expression anywhere to be seen. :(

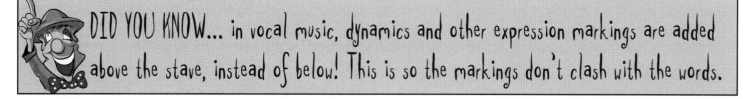

DID YOU KNOW... in vocal music, dynamics and other expression markings are added above the stave, instead of below! This is so the markings don't clash with the words.

# Setting Words to Music

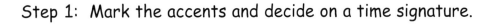

Now it's your turn to set words to music. In Grade 4 you had lots of practice setting verse to a rhythm... now we just need to go a step further, and set that rhythm to a melody!

Here is a simple couplet:

> Ring out the bells, start up the fun,
> Show all the beauty around.
>
> (A bit corny, but this is the kind of stuff you get in the exam!)

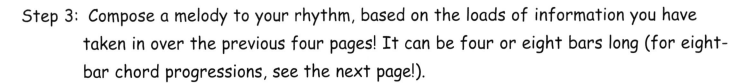

Step 1: Mark the accents and decide on a time signature.

Step 2: Compose an interesting rhythm that suits the words.

Step 3: Compose a melody to your rhythm, based on the loads of information you have taken in over the previous four pages! It can be four or eight bars long (for eight-bar chord progressions, see the next page!).

Let's revise a few quick tips:

★ Begin and end with chord I.
★ Aim for chord V at the end of the first phrase (i.e. at the end of the first line of poetry).
★ Be careful with the leading note – it should resolve to the tonic (if it's not part of a scale passage).
★ Aim for a nice mixture of passing notes and chord jumps.

Write your melody here in F major, writing the words clearly underneath the notes:

Awesome work! Finally, you need to add some extra performance markings, like phrasing, dynamics, and a tempo marking. Then it will be ready for a singer to perform!

# Guidelines for Great Melodies

← →

★ The first and last bars should be based on chord I. The melody may begin on any note of chord I, but **the last note must be the tonic.**

★ Make sure you reach chord V at the halfway point, giving it that unfinished feeling.

★ **Never leap to/from the leading note, unless it is to/from another note of chord V.**

★ The leading note should go **up** to the tonic, unless it is part of a descending scale passage.

★ **Never leap to or from a passing note, and avoid passing notes on strong beats.**

★ For an anacrusis, choose a note from chord V. For a two-note anacrusis, you could use scale degrees 5–4 (going to the mediant) or 3–2 (going to the tonic).

★ If you are in a minor key, remember to raise the leading note, BUT... (see next point)

★ Avoid the augmented 2nd between scale degrees 6 and 7 in minor keys. Use the melodic form of the minor scale.

★ A leap of a 6th or 8ve can sound really good! (But don't use too many.) The notes immediately following the leap should move in the **opposite** direction to the leap.

---

## Good Chord Progressions

Composing a melody is easiest if you base it on chords. Below are three ideas for eight-bar chord progressions. (If you are composing a four-bar melody, just use two chords per bar!)

| Bar 1 | Bar 2 | Bar 3 | Bar 4 | Bar 5 | Bar 6 | Bar 7 | Bar 8 |
|-------|-------|-------|-------|-------|-------|-------|-------|
| I | IV | II | V | I | II | V | I |
| I | II | IV | V | I | IV | V | I |
| I | VI* | II | V | VI* | II | V | I |

*We haven't studied chord VI yet, but it sounds wonderful in melodies. Discuss chord VI with your teacher before you use it!

# Creative Couplets

$\longleftrightarrow$

Here are a few couplets for you to set to music. Compose a rhythm first, decide on a nice chord progression (see previous page) then write the melody. Don't forget to add phrasing, dynamics and a tempo marking!

1.     I wish that I was wealthy, I wish that I could fly
       Away to far-off places, to mountain tops so high.

Graeme Watt

2.     When it comes to shearing, a lotta tales are spun,
       Some boasting is in earnest and some of it's in fun.

Anon

3.     I'm the monarch of valley, and hill, and plain,
       And the king of this golden land.

Thomas E. Spencer

4.     Across a strip of pasture land, when washing day is fine,
       I sometimes watch my neighbour's wife hang garments on the line.

J.W. Gordon

5.     The little fairy penguin who zooms about the ocean,
       On terra firma travels with an awkward waddling motion.

Jim Haynes

6.     I live in the shades where the honey-bells grow.
       I sing in the sunlight; I sleep in the snow.

Charles Souter

7.     No drums were beat, no trumpets blared, the day they marched away;
       Their wives and sweethearts watched them go and none would bid them stay!

Charles Souter

For extra practice: Make up two or more melodies for each couplet!

# Let's Get Back to Cadences

As you learned over the last few pages, melodies are often based on chords, and some of those chords form cadences. Can you identify the perfect, plagal and imperfect cadences in this music by Purcell? The key is.... well, you can work out the key. (Go back to page 43 to check out which chords make up which cadences)

Cadence X:_____        Cadence Y:_____   Cadence Z:_____

Good work! In your exam it's a little different... rather than actually naming or identifying cadences, you have to choose which chords will sound best under certain melody notes. For example, you'll get a melody with sets of bracketed notes, like this:

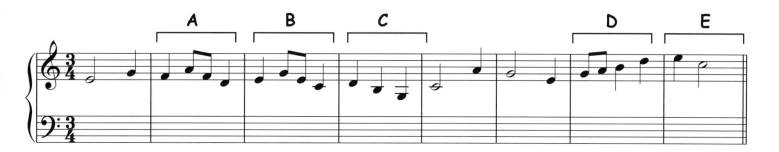

Step 1: Identify the key of the melody (C, G, F, or D major): _____

Step 2: On some spare paper, write a chord grid in that key.

Step 3: Find the chord that contains the **majority** of the notes under each bracket.

Once you've decided on which chords will fit, you can either write the chord numbers here:

Chord A: _____        Chord B: _____        Chord C: _____        Chord D: _____        Chord E: _____

**OR** you can actually draw the notes of the chord (in root position) on the bass stave – it's completely up to you! On the next page you'll find out what this has to do with cadences...

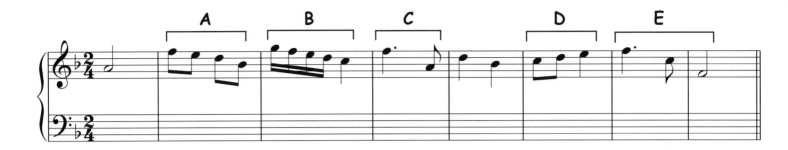

In your exam, the place to write your answers will be listed under two headings, 'First Cadence' and 'Second Cadence'. The last two chords in each set must form a perfect, imperfect or plagal cadence.

Write your answers here (after going through steps 1–3 on the previous page, of course), listing the chords that suit the example above:

FIRST CADENCE

Chord A: _____

Chord B: _____

Chord C: _____

SECOND CADENCE

Chord D: _____

Chord E: _____

 HERE'S A THOUGHT... In a group of three chords, the first of the three chords is called the **approach chord** and the next two chords form the actual cadence.

Sometimes more than one chord will suit the note or notes under each bracket. You have to make a decision which is best, and this is where your knowledge of cadences really kicks in!

★ Remember there is no such thing as a cadence that ends on II or IV.

★ If you have a choice between chords II and IV, it's a safe choice to go with chord IV. Remember there is no such cadence as II – I!

FIRST CADENCE

Chord A: _____

Chord B: _____

SECOND CADENCE

Chord C: _____

Chord D: _____

Chord E: _____

# Practice Makes Perfect (and imperfect and plagal ha ha)

For each of these, identify the key and use chord grids to help you decide on the chords.

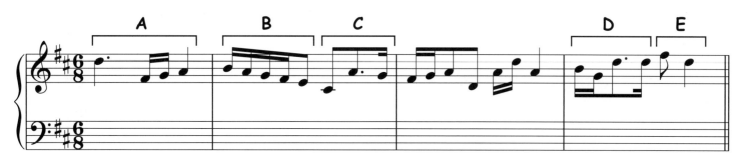

FIRST CADENCE

Chord A: _____

Chord B: _____

SECOND CADENCE

Chord C: _____

Chord D: _____

Chord E: _____

FIRST CADENCE

Chord A: _____

Chord B: _____

Chord C: _____

SECOND CADENCE

Chord D: _____

Chord E: _____

FIRST CADENCE

Chord A: _____

Chord B: _____

SECOND CADENCE

Chord C: _____

Chord D: _____

Chord E: _____

53

# Continuing a Motif

The exam question gives you a choice between setting a verse to melody OR continuing a given motif to write for an instrument. The advantages of continuing a motif over setting poetry to music are:

★ You are not restricted by words/mood of poetry.

★ The first phrase is all done for you! The rhythmic and melodic idea has been established and it's up to you to continue in the same style.

★ You've had LOADS of experience writing rhythms based on given openings, so you just need to go one step further and set that rhythm to a melody!

A good way to approach this is to think of the given motif as a 'question'.

Here is a question in B minor:

So now we need an 'answer'. Here are three ideas:

1.    This answer reinforces the rhythmic ideas in the question.

2.    This answer provides a rhythmic contrast to the question.

3.    This answer could probably do with some spicing up!

All three of these answers end on a note from chord V. Remember, it's important to reach chord V halfway through your melody! (Revise all the melody writing tips on page 49) Choose one of the answers above and write it after the question on the next page.

Your question (Q) and answer (A) can now form the basis of the second half of your melody. You could bring back a slightly varied question in bars 5 and 6 (we'll call this Q2) and use ideas from the answer to compose bars 7 and 8 (let's call it A2).

Remember, melodies work best when based on **chords**. Compose bars 5-8 now:

So, your eight-bar melody has a formula of **Q – A – Q2 – A2**. Here are some other formulas you can try. Compose another melody based on the same motif, choosing one of these:

★Q - Q2 - A - A2★     ★Q - A - Q - Q2★          ★Q - Q2 - Q3 - A★

Which instrument is your melody best suited to? (See instrument ranges pages 63–67) _____
Now it's time to add some performance markings for that instrument, as well as all the usual phrasing and expression markings!

Here is another motif. Use this as the opening to write a melody for either violin or flute. Add a tempo marking, phrasing, and dynamics. Keep to the range of your chosen instrument.

Go back to page 49 and read up on some great melody-writing hints and chord progressions, then go forward to pages 63–67 to learn about the range and special performance markings for each instrument. Once you've done all that, come back to this page and continue each of these openings to make balanced eight-bar melodies. Add tempo markings, phrasing and dynamics, and don't forget to think in 'question' and 'answer' formulas!

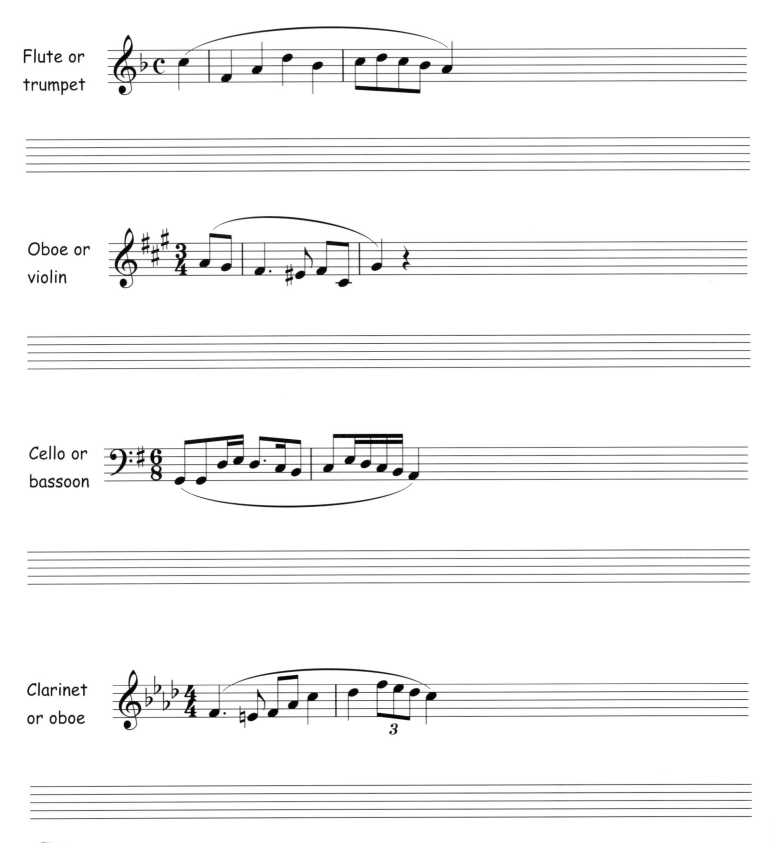

 Go to www.blitzbooks.com for more excellent tips on melody writing, including a great worksheet on sequences!

# Exam-Style Melody Page

**EITHER***

Compose a melody to the following words for solo voice. Write each syllable clearly under the notes. Include a tempo marking and other appropriate performance directions.

> Green and amber and gold it grows
>
> When the sun sinks late in the West

A.B. Paterson

**OR****

Continue this opening to write a melody for unaccompanied bassoon or cello. Your complete melody should be eight bars long. Include a tempo marking and other appropriate performance directions.

\* Just kidding. Today you have to do both of these exercises, for practice. But you WILL get to choose one or the other in your exam!

\*\* Like I said, just kidding.

# Ornaments

In Grade 4 you had to recognise and name ornaments. In Grade 5 you also need the skill of replacing the actual sound with the correct ornament!

| Actual Sound | Replace with | Name of Ornament |
|---|---|---|
| | | Upper mordent (no vertical line) / Lower mordent (with vertical line) |
| | | Trill (or 'shake') |
| | | Acciaccatura or 'crushed note' (little line through tail) |
| | | Appoggiatura or 'leaning note' (no line through tail) |
| | | Turn |
| | | Turn (between notes) |
| | | Arpeggiation (or 'fanning' of the notes) |

Other things to know:

★ Ornaments may have accidentals, e.g.

★ When you draw a turn, think of it as a backwards 'S' lying on its side! ∾

★ Two or more grace notes look like this:     . They can be played as acciaccaturas (crushed notes) or appoggiaturas (leaning notes), depending on the style of music!

# Reiterations and Repeats

Composers use shortcuts when notes, bars, phrases and sections of music are repeated. You already know quite a few of these, like the repeat dots at a double bar, 'D.C. al fine', the 'dal segno' sign ( 𝄋 ), that sort of thing. But here are a few you may not have seen before!

| Written | Played | Written | Played |
|---|---|---|---|

There are even repeat signs for whole bars of music:

Repeat the previous bar

Repeat the previous two bars

Let's test your skills. Check out this music by Wagner:

★ Write a sign here that could replace all the notes in bar 2. _____

★ Write bar 1 as it would sound: _____

★ True or false: This entire melody is to be repeated. _____

# Quick Quiz

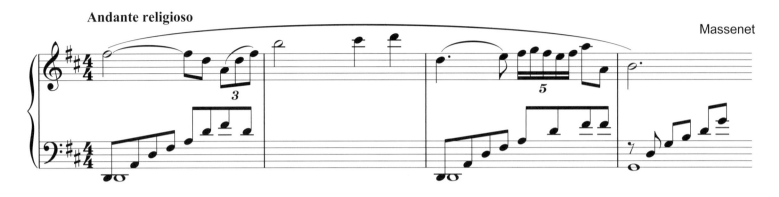

Andante religioso

Massenet

1. Add an ornament to make this bar sound the same as bar 3.

2. Draw a sign in bar 2 of the bass stave to show that it is a repeat of bar 1.

3. How many demisemiquavers is the quintuplet in bar 3 worth? ___

4. What does 'andante religioso' mean? _____
   ('Religioso' is not on your list of terms, but you could have a good pretty good guess)

5. Rewrite the treble melody one octave lower, using the alto clef.



6. What is the currency of New Zealand? _____ (not essential Grade 5 knowledge)

7. Rewrite the following music by Scarlatti with correct grouping/beaming of notes and
   rests (it's been a while since you've been tested on this, lucky you).

# Terms

←→

Notice how this page is not called 'Italian Terms'? That's because there are some GERMAN terms to learn in Grade 5 as well as Italian! (Lucky you) Remember, you need to know these **in addition to** all the terms you learned in Grades 1–4. Find them all at **www.blitzbooks.com**, and you can also check out **How to Blitz! Musical Knowledge.**

## Italian

| | | |
|---|---|---|
| *attacca* | - | go on at once |
| *dolente* | - | mournful, sad |
| *dolore, doloroso* | - | grief, sorrowful |
| *doppio movimento* | - | twice as fast |
| *estinto* | - | lifeless |
| *incalzando* | - | getting quicker |
| *lacrimoso* | - | sad |
| *loco* | - | at normal pitch |
| *lunga* | - | long (e.g. for a pause) |
| *lusingando* | - | in a persuasive style |
| *misura* | - | measure |
| *ossia* | - | or, alternative |
| *piacevole* | - | pleasant |
| *piangevole* | - | plaintive |
| *pochettino (poch.)* | - | rather little |
| *rinforzando (rf, rfz)* | - | reinforced sound |
| *smorzando (smorz.)* | - | dying away (volume and tempo) |
| *teneramente* | - | tenderly |
| *tenerezza* | - | tenderness |
| *tosto* | - | swift |
| *volante* | - | flying (fast) |

## German

| | | |
|---|---|---|
| *aber* | - | but |
| *bewegt* | - | with quick movement, agitated |
| *breit* | - | broad |
| *ein* | - | one |
| *einfach* | - | simple |
| *etwas* | - | somewhat |
| *fröhlich* | - | cheerful, joyful |
| *immer* | - | always |
| *langsam* | - | slow |
| *lebhaft* | - | lively |
| *mässig* | - | at a moderate speed |
| *mit Ausdruck* | - | with expression |
| *nicht* | - | not |
| *ohne* | - | without |
| *ruhig* | - | at a moderate speed |
| *schnell* | - | fast |
| *sehr* | - | very |
| *süss* | - | sweet |
| *traurig* | - | sad |
| *und* | - | and |
| *voll* | - | full |
| *wenig* | - | little |
| *wieder* | - | again |
| *zart* | - | tender, delicate |
| *zu* | - | too |

# Tiny Test

1. Translate these German instructions:

   *mit Ausdruck aber nicht zu schnell* _____

   *langsam und immer sehr ruhig* _____

2. Here is some music by Chopin, followed by (surprise, surprise) some exercises relating to it:

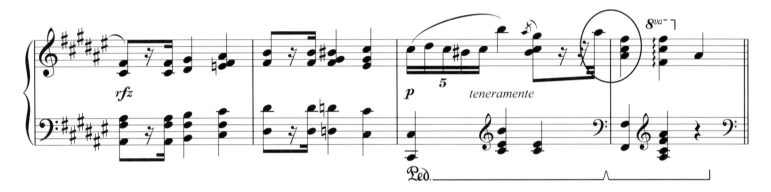

★ What key is it in? The last note is the mediant. _____

★ What does '*rfz*' stand for and what does it mean? _____

★ What does '*teneramente*' mean? _____

★ The quintuplet in bar 3 is the written form of which ornament? _____

★ Add an ornament to this chord which would make it
  sound the same as the circled notes in bars 3-4.

★ Add a sign to show that the last chord in the left hand should be arpeggiated.

★ Add an Italian term to show that the last treble note should be played at normal pitch.

3. Fill in this table with matching terms in each of three languages (wow, you're multilingual now!):

| FRENCH | GERMAN | ITALIAN |
|--------|--------|---------|
| *cédez* |  | *ritardando* |
|  | *langsam* |  |
|  |  | *meno* |
|  | *ruhig* |  |
| *très* |  |  |

62

# The String Family

| Instrument | Approximate Range | Common Terms and Signs | Interesting Facts About Strings |
|---|---|---|---|
| Violin | | *con sordino*: play with mute<br><br>*sul ponticello*: play on or near the bridge<br><br>V up bow<br><br>⊓ down bow<br><br>*arco*: with the bow<br><br>*pizzicato*: pluck the strings<br><br>*sul G*: play on the G string<br><br>double-stopping: playing two or more notes at once | ★ The bow is drawn across the strings to make them vibrate and produce sound<br><br>★ Double bass music is written an octave higher than it sounds<br><br>★ The full name for cello is actually 'violoncello'<br><br>★ A slur over the notes indicates to play in one bow<br><br>★ The open strings of the violin, viola and cello are all a 5th apart<br><br>★ The open strings of a double bass are a 4th apart |
| Viola | | | |
| Cello | | | |
| Double Bass | | | |

Insert the correct sign where indicated:

Bach

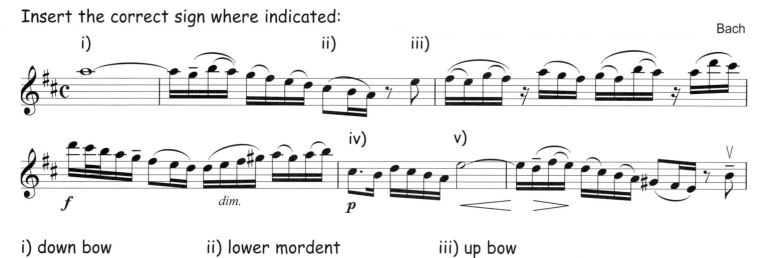

i) down bow            ii) lower mordent            iii) up bow

iv) a direction to pluck the strings            v) a direction to play with the bow

63

# The Woodwind Family

| Instrument | Approximate Written Range | Common Terms and Signs | Interesting Facts About Woodwinds |
|---|---|---|---|
| Piccolo | | Flutter tonguing | ★ Air is blown across or into the mouthpiece or reed to make the column of air vibrate. |
| Flute | | , (breath mark) | ★ The piccolo sounds an octave higher than written. |
| Oboe | | | ★ Flute and piccolo are the only non-reed instruments. |
| Clarinet | | | ★ The oboe, cor anglais and bassoon are double-reed instruments. |
| Bass Clarinet | | | ★ The clarinet is a single-reed instrument. |
| Cor Anglais | | | ★ The bass clarinet sounds one octave lower than the B♭ clarinet. |
| | | | ★ All clarinets are notated within the same written range, and all in treble clef. |
| Bassoon | | | ★ The bassoon and contrabassoon often use tenor clef. |
| | | | ★ The contrabassoon sounds one octave lower than written. |
| Contrabassoon (or double bassoon) | | | ★ The saxophone is another single-reed woodwind instrument but is not usually in an orchestra. |

# The Brass Family

⟵⟶

| Instrument | Approximate Written Range | Interesting Facts About Brass | Common Terms and Signs |
|---|---|---|---|
| Trumpet | | ★ The brass section use mutes, but they are very different to string mutes. They are conical objects that are inserted into the bell of the instrument. | *con sordino*: play with mute **fp** *(forte-piano)*: loud then immediately soft |
| Horn | | ★ The horn is the only brass instrument included in a wind quintet (along with flute, oboe, clarinet and bassoon). ★ The horn, trombone and tuba are also known as the French horn, tenor trombone and bass tuba. | |
| Trombone | | Tuba | |

Here is the theme from Mozart's famous horn concerto. Answer the questions below:

*senza sordino*

★ What does *senza sordino* mean? _____

★ Bar 5 is a repeat of bar 1. Write it as it will sound.

# The Percussion Family

| UNPITCHED PERCUSSION | | |
| --- | --- | --- |
| **Instrument** | **Common Terms and Signs** | **Interesting Facts About Percussion** |
| Cymbals | Roll (like a trill)<br><br>✗ (unpitched notehead) | ★ Most percussion instruments are struck with sticks or mallets (or against each other, as with cymbals).<br><br>★ Other unpitched percussion instruments also found in the orchestra include castanets and bongo drums. |
| Side drum | | |
| Bass drum | | |
| Triangle | | |

| PITCHED PERCUSSION | | |
| --- | --- | --- |
| **Instrument** | **Common Terms and Signs** | **Interesting Facts About Percussion** |
| Timpani | Roll (like a trill) | ★ Other pitched percussion instruments also found in the orchestra include tubular bells and chime bars. |
| Xylophone | | |
| Glockenspiel | | |
| Marimba | | |

# The Keyboard Family

| Instrument | Common Terms and Signs | Interesting Facts About Keyboard Instruments |
|---|---|---|
| Piano | *una corda (u.c.)* ('one string'): depress the soft pedal<br><br>*tre corde (t.c.)* ('three strings'): release the soft pedal<br><br>*m.s/m.d*: 'left hand'/'right hand' (Italian)<br><br>*m.g/m.d*: 'left hand'/'right hand' (French) | ★ The first pianos were made in Italy in the early 1700s. Using hammers to strike the strings, they gave performers close control over a wide range of dynamics. Upright pianos came along around 100 years later.<br><br>★ Modern pianos usually have 88 keys, giving just over seven octaves. Most have at least two pedals – a 'soft' pedal and a 'sustain' pedal – and some might have a 'sostenuto' pedal, which allows the performer to choose which notes to sustain, or a very quiet 'practice' pedal. |
| Organ | | |
| Harpsichord | Harp* | Celesta |

*Harp is not really a keyboard instrument but it has a range similar to piano. It is an orchestral instrument most often associated with the strings section.

Here is some piano music by Moszkowski that features many of the signs listed above. Discuss each one of these with your teacher!

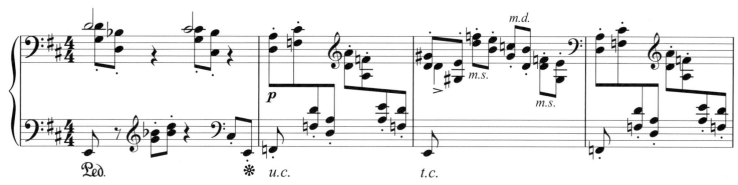

# Crossword

Wow, you have certainly learned a lot in this book, especially in the last few pages! It's time to put your knowledge to the test (but not a very serious test). Complete the crossword below by solving the 'across' and 'down' clues. Have fun!

## Across

1. Term for bowing two strings at once
9. Piccolo music sounds this much higher than written
11. Clef often used by cello and bassoon
13. G♯ is the _____ equivalent of A♭
14. Music for B flat instruments must be transposed ___ __ _____ (2, 1, 4)
17. Italian term for 'alternative part'
19. Make sure you add these to your melody, as well as articulation and phrasing

20. Interval spanning more than an octave

25. The strings of a bow are actually made of these, from a horse's tail

26. Highest female voice

28. Name of 'The Magic Dragon'

29. The writing of SATB voices on four separate staves

30. Number and type of this interval:

33. Something no teenager can do without

35. Family of instruments to which the celesta belongs

36. Unlike the rest of the string family, the double bass is tuned in _____

37. Very low bassoon

38. German term for 'little'

# Down

2. G, D, A and E are the _____ string tunings of the violin

3. English meaning of 'breit'

4. You must do this to written music for clarinet otherwise it will sound wrong with piano

5. Non-transposing instruments sound at concert _____

6. In Grade 5 you need to know Italian, French and _____ terms

7. Type of this 6th:

8. Italian term for 'go straight on'

10. Alto clef and tenor clef are both also known as a _____

12. Brass instrument that sometimes uses tenor clef

15. The clarinet in A sounds this much lower than written

16. Male voice in between bass and tenor

18. Relative of the oboe

21. Type of scale with a raised 6th and 7th ascending

22. Time signatures with 5, 7 or 8 as the top number are known as this

23. These are used to raise the leading notes in G♯ and D♯ minor

24. Scale degree no. 2

26. $\frac{6}{4}$ chords are in this inversion

27. Key with six flats (doesn't matter whether you pick major or minor)

31. German term for 'at a moderate speed'

32. Lower type of soprano voice/Italian for 'medium'

34. Italian abbreviation for 'held back'

# Use Your Skills

It's time to answer more questions about lots of different excerpts of music. Have fun!

Fauré

★ Insert the missing time signature.

★ Name and explain the squiggly line on the first chord of the piano part:

_____

★ Why is the solo part in a different key from the piano part? _____

_____

★ The key is E♭ major. Name the chord number and inversion of the circled chord in bar 9: _____

★ Give the English meaning of the following terms:

*rf*  _____

*volante*  _____

**Tosto**  _____

70

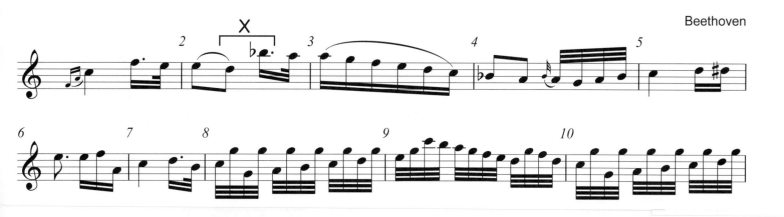

Beethoven

★ Name the ornament in bar 4: _____

★ Rewrite bar 2, replacing the first two notes with an ornament:

★ Insert the time signature.

★ Bar 7 should sound like this: Add the missing ornament above.

★ What is the value of the last note of bar 1? _____

★ Fully describe the interval marked X: _____

★ Put a bracket over four consecutive notes that form a chromatic scale.

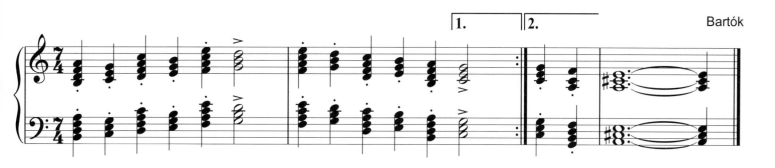

Bartók

★ Explain the signs [1.] [2.] _____

★ For how many beats will the last chord sound? _____

★ How many different types of repeat signs are in this extract? _____

★ Name two instruments that could play this music: _____

★ Add an Italian term to show that the second bar should be played twice as fast.

★ Rewrite the last chord of the right hand in the tenor clef:

71

★ Name two keys that share the key signature of this piece: _____

★ How many double flats are in this excerpt? _____

★ Explain the tempo marking: _____

★ Explain '*m.d.*' (bar 2): _____

★ Explain how the last five semiquavers in bar 3 are to be played: _____

_____

★ Rewrite the circled chord in bar 4 enharmonically, without accidentals: ═══════════

★ True or false: Hermione Granger's parents were dentists. _____

★ There is a change of time signature in bar 6. Insert the correct one.

★ Insert the missing rest/s at the place marked with an asterisk in bar 6.

Satie

Nicht schnell

★ This music is written for a solo transposing woodwind instrument with piano accompaniment. Name the solo instrument: _____

★ Which bars contain irregular subdivisions? _____

★ How many semiquavers is the circled note in bar 6 worth? _____

★ How many bars feature demisemiquavers? _____

★ Rewrite bar 4 (solo part) at concert pitch:

★ How many times does the tonic chord feature in the piano part? (It's in a major key) ____

★ Explain the tempo marking: _____

73

# Test Paper... Sort Of

All theory books end with a test paper, but this one is DIFFERENT. It already has the answers in it (mostly wrong answers!) and your job is to be the teacher – you have to **mark** it.

When you've found all the mistakes, go to **www.blitzbooks.com** and download the EXACT SAME PAPER – this time with no answers already in it. See if you can get 100%!

★ ★ ★ ★ ★ ★ ★

**Theory Paper Grade 5**

**Time allowed: 2 hours**

TOTAL MARKS
100

1    Study this extract by Albéniz and then answer the questions below.

15

a)    What is the meaning of 'dolente'? ...*Sweetly*........................................    (2)

b)    Insert the correct time signature.    (2)

c)    Name two keys that share the key signature of this extract. ...*E maj*...... and ...*C min*.... (2)

d)    True or false: the last bar contains the sound of a G natural. ......*False*......    (1)

e)    Fully describe the circled interval in bar 2. *A fourth between E + B with a*    (2)
      *sharp on the E and both quavers*

f)    Rewrite the first chord of the left-hand (bass) part in the tenor clef at the same pitch.    (3)
      Remember to write the key signature.

g)    Underline the instruments that could play this piece:    (3)

**violin**          **piano**              **timpani**          **organ**          **celesta**

74

**2**      Describe fully (e.g. major 2nd) each of the bracketed melodic intervals below.    (10)

Paganini

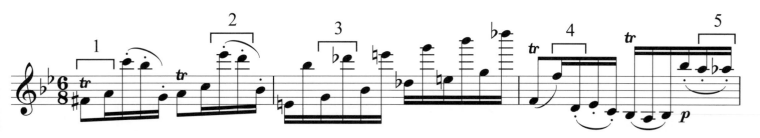

Intervals:

1    Minor 3rd

2    Major 2nd

3    Diminished 11th

4    Minor 3rd

5    Minor 2nd

**3**      The following melody is written for clarinet in B flat. Transpose it down    (10)
a major 2nd, as will sound at concert pitch. Do not use a key signature, but
add all necessary accidentals.

Leoncavallo

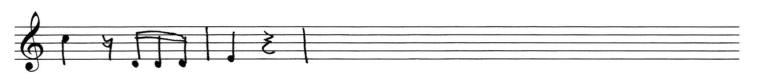

**4** Study this music by Schumann and answer the questions that follow.

i) This music is written for one stringed instrument and one keyboard instrument. (2)

Name the two most likely. ......Piano............ and ........viola................

ii) Name three different ornaments in this piece, stating the bar in which each occurs. (6)

Ornament ......trill............ Ornament ......trill............ Ornament ......mordent........

Bar ....4........ Bar ....5........ Bar ....7........

iii) Rewrite the circled chord in bar 3 so that it sounds at the same pitch, but using the tenor (4)
C clef. Remember to write the clef and the key signature.

iv) Explain the 𝄻_____ sign under bar 5. ...Ped = foot, so use your foot..... (2)

v) Describe the chords marked X and Y in bar 4 as I, II, IV or V in the key of F major. (4)
Also indicate whether the lowest note of the chord is the root (a), 3rd (b) or 5th (c).

X ...... I a .........

Y ...... IV a .....

vi) Give the English meaning of: (6)

**Mit Ausdruck** ...... with feeling ......

*fp* (bar 1) ... loud and soft at the same time ...

*cresc.* (bar 4)...... crescendo ......

vii) Give the name of the voice part that lies between soprano and alto in vocal range. (2)

............ Sopralto ............

viii) Underline one instrument below that is a member of the orchestral brass family. (2)

oboe          <u>french horn</u          tambourine          celesta

ix) Name two instruments from the woodwind family that use bass clef. (2)

............ Bassoon and bass clarinet ............

77

**5** a) Write the key signature of five sharps and then one octave descending of the melodic minor scale with that key signature.

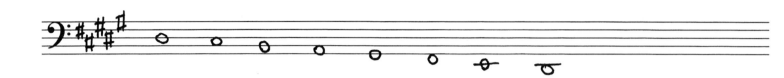

b) Place accidentals in front of any necessary notes in order to form a G♭ chromatic scale. Do not use a key signature.

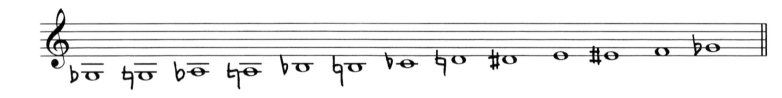

## 6    EITHER

a)    Compose a balanced eight-bar melody (unaccompanied) for violin or trumpet, using the opening given below. Include the tempo and other performance directions, in particular any that might be specific to your chosen instrument.

Instrument for which the melody is written: ........................................

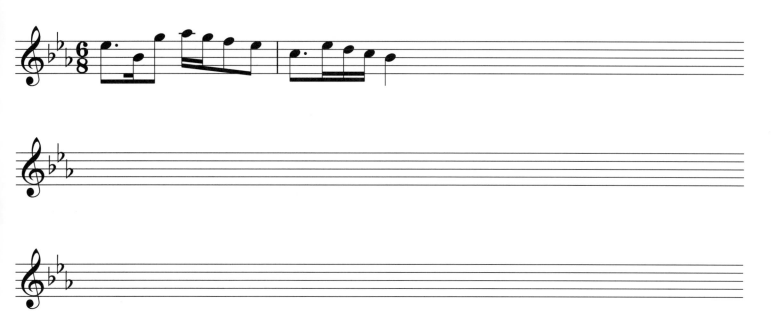

**OR**

b)    Compose a melody to the following words, for solo voice. Write each syllable clearly under the notes. Also indicate the tempo and other performance directions.

She sits beside the tinted tide,

That's reddened by the tortured sand      Lawson

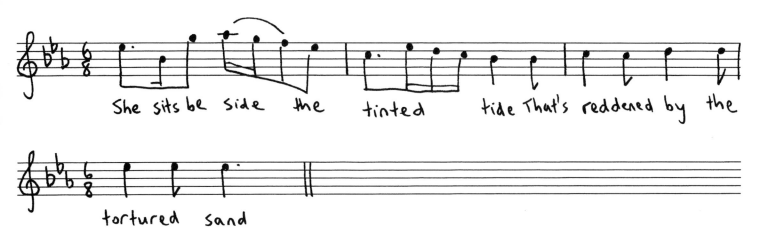

7    Suggest chord progressions for two cadences in the following melody by
     writing chord I, II, IV or V at each of the places marked A-E below. You do
     not have to specify the position of the chords.

     Indicate the chords by either of these methods:

     a)    writing I, II etc. or any other recognised symbols on the dotted lines below, OR

     b)    write notes on the staves

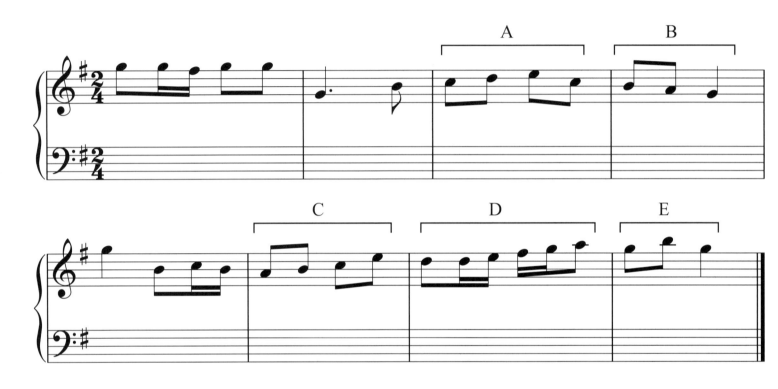

FIRST CADENCE:

Chord A    .........IV....................

Chord B    .........I....................

SECOND CADENCE:

Chord C    .........II..or..IV.....

Chord D    .........V....................

Chord E    .........I....................

How did you do marking this paper? Did you find lots of mistakes? Now go to www.blitzbooks.com and download the uncompleted version. Good luck!